When Jeremiah A Learned A Secret

Words by Norman C. Habel
Pictures by Jim Roberts

Concordia Publishing House

A PURPLE PUZZLE TREE BOOK

COPYRIGHT © 1972 CONCORDIA PUBLISHING HOUSE, ST. LOUIS, MISSOURI
CONCORDIA PUBLISHING HOUSE LTD., LONDON, E. C. 1
MANUFACTURED IN THE UNITED STATES OF AMERICA
ALL RIGHTS RESERVED
ISBN 0-570-06525-9

OTHER TITLES

SET I.
WHEN GOD WAS ALL ALONE 56-1200
WHEN THE FIRST MAN CAME 56-1201
IN THE ENCHANTED GARDEN 56-1202
WHEN THE PURPLE WATERS CAME AGAIN 56-1203
IN THE LAND OF THE GREAT WHITE CASTLE 56-1204
WHEN LAUGHING BOY WAS BORN 56-1205
SET I LP RECORD 79-2200
SET I GIFT BOX (6 BOOKS, 1 RECORD) 56-1206

SET II.
HOW TRICKY JACOB WAS TRICKED 56-1207
WHEN JACOB BURIED HIS TREASURE 56-1208
WHEN GOD TOLD US HIS NAME 56-1209
IS THAT GOD AT THE DOOR? 56-1210
IN THE MIDDLE OF A WILD CHASE 56-1211
THIS OLD MAN CALLED MOSES 56-1212
SET II LP RECORD 79-2201
SET II GIFT BOX (6 BOOKS, 1 RECORD) 56-1213

SET III.
THE TROUBLE WITH TICKLE THE TIGER 56-1218
AT THE BATTLE OF JERICHO! HO! HO! 56-1219
GOD IS NOT A JACK-IN-A-BOX 56-1220
A LITTLE BOY WHO HAD A LITTLE FLING 56-1221
THE KING WHO WAS A CLOWN 56-1222
SING A SONG OF SOLOMON 56-1223
SET III LP RECORD 79-2202
SET III GIFT BOX (6 BOOKS, 1 RECORD) 56-1224

SET IV.
ELIJAH AND THE BULL-GOD BAAL 56-1225
LONELY ELIJAH AND THE LITTLE PEOPLE 56-1226
WHEN ISAIAH SAW THE SIZZLING SERAPHIM 56-1227
A VOYAGE TO THE BOTTOM OF THE SEA 56-1228
WHEN JEREMIAH LEARNED A SECRET 56-1229
THE CLUMSY ANGEL AND THE NEW KING 56-1230
SET IV LP RECORD 79-2203
SET IV GIFT BOX (6 BOOKS, 1 RECORD) 56-1231

the PURPLE PUZZLE TREE

Jeremiah was sad and lonely.
He wandered slowly through his city
and kicked the ashes
of burnt beds and broken toys
that once were bright and pretty.

He was looking for a pot
he had hidden near his home
in the city of Jerusalem
that was now a pile of stones.

As he poked through the rubble,
he found a broken flask
that once was long and lovely
like a very pretty vase.

As he picked up the pieces,
he remembered something sad
that had happened years before.
For one day God told Jeremiah
to buy a beautiful flask
with his very own money.
He had to do a job for God
that wasn't very funny.

He stood beside the city gate
and yelled his wild, wild words.
"God will take your town," he cried,
"and smash it all to bits."
"You think the house of God won't fall,
for that's where Yahweh sits?
Well, He will smash the temple, too,
as if it were a flask,
and no matter how you try,
you'll never find the parts."

Why do you think that God
would do a thing like that?

Jeremiah took the precious flask
and slowly raised his hand.
Then with a blast
he flung the flask
hard upon the ground.

The priests were very angry.
They grabbed poor Jeremiah.
They threw him in the stocks
with chains around his feet,
and jammed his head
between two wooden blocks.
As everybody passed,
they hissed and spat and laughed
at lonely Jeremiah.

Well, Jeremiah's words came true,
and Jerusalem was broken like a pot.
But no one said, "Well, you were right!"
They only said, "So what?"

As he wandered through the ashes,
he found a piece of wood
that used to be a yoke for cows
to wear across their necks
when they pulled their carts or plows.

As he held that piece of wood,
he remembered something sad
that had happened years before.
For one day God told Jeremiah
to make a wooden yoke
and wear it round his neck.

So Jeremiah made the yoke
with bars and leather thongs
and wore it on his neck.
He went to see the king
and tell him what it meant.
"This wooden yoke
is not a joke," he said.
"But like a cow
that pulls a plow,
you'll soon be bound like slaves.
The mighty king of Babylon
will kidnap all of you."

Why do you think that Jeremiah
would say a thing like that?

Well, Jeremiah's words were true,
and the king of Babylon came.
But no one said, "Well, you were right!"
They only said, "We're not to blame!"

When the king of Babylon arrived,
he broke through the walls.
He killed a lot of people
and kidnapped many more.

Then he did a deed so cruel
it's hard to even say.
He burnt the lovely city down
as if the homes were hay.

Do you know how it feels
to watch your home burn down?
Do you know what it's like
when your toys and clothes,
your books and games,
are lost forever,
burnt by hungry flames?

Jeremiah wandered through the ashes
looking for his pot.
And suddenly, there it was,
like a jewel in the rubble!
As he picked up the pot,
he remembered something good
that had happened just last year.

One day, when all the soldiers
were standing on the walls,
fighting mighty Babylon
with spears and stones and balls,
the prophet did a strange thing.

He called his cousin down
to the middle of the street.
And there he bought from him
a little block of land.
Everybody laughed aloud,
for everything would soon belong
to the mighty king of Babylon,
who was greedy, fierce, and proud.

But Jeremiah took a scroll
and made some people sign it
to prove the land was his.
Then he took that scroll,
with its special secret words,
and sealed it in a pot
hidden in a hole.

Jeremiah sat among the ashes
with the scroll between his hands.
It was really like a precious piece
of God's special puzzle plan.

Then Jeremiah read the secret
he had written in that scroll.
Its message was a letter
from God to all His people
who were slaves in Babylon.

"Dear slaves," He said,
"I burnt your lovely city
    because you loved it more than Me.
I kidnapped you from home
    because you loved it more than Me.
But now I'll change your heart
    to love Me once again.
I'll bring you home with Me
    to build My puzzle plan.
And that little plot of land
    that Jeremiah bought
will be the very place
    where I will come again
    to solve My puzzle plan."